THEY'RE ALL
GOING TO LAUGH AT YOU

By

Trarina Paige

They're All Going to Laugh At You

Proverbs 17:22 A merry heart doeth good like a medicine...
– This is the story of Grace Wilson who finds great purpose
in bringing joy to people around the world.

Life is worth living as long as there's a laugh in it."
– L.M. MONTGOMERY, ANNE OF GREEN GABLES

Dedication

I would like to dedicate this book to my amazing children.
You guys motivate me to go after my dreams.

So here's to you KIDS.

Ever since she could remember, Grace loved bringing joy into people's hearts and creating giant smiles on their faces.

The greatest feeling came from brightening up someone's day—friend, family, or a random stranger alike!

Even as a little child, Grace went out of her way to turn a frown upside down. One day, a little boy was crying at daycare.

He didn't want his mother to leave, so Grace walked over to sit beside him. She made silly faces and funny fart sounds until he finally smiled.

Grace amazing sense of humor is how she met her best friend, Jana who sat by herself during recess.

As Jana looked down, a cheerful voice yelled out towards her, "Knock! Knock!"

"Who's there?" Jana softly replied.

"Ice cream," said Grace.

"Ice cream who?" Jana replied.

"ICE CREAM SO YOU CAN HEAR ME!"

Grace always knew how to lift everyone's spirits. However, that changed one day during math class.

Grace and her classmates worked on an assignment with Mrs. Henderson, a very focused teacher who wanted the best from her students.

Mrs. Henderson called on a new student named Johnny. He stood quietly at the board with a piece of chalk shaking in his hand.

Wanting to make everyone more comfortable, Grace decided to distract everyone with a joke.

"HEYYYY!" Grace yelled. "What did one toilet say to the other? You look a bit flushed!"

Everyone laughed, except Mrs. Henderson.

Grace's joke had worked to help Johnny,
but it landed her in big trouble.

"Why is everything a joke with you?"
Mrs. Henderson asked.

Grace replied, "I love laughter!
It brings joy to everyone's heart."

"Well, if you want to be successful in life,
you need to leave the jokes behind you!
No one will ever take a funny
girl seriously!"

For the rest of the day, Grace sat
in silence. She wondered what
Mrs. Henderson meant about
no one taking her seriously.

Could she not be successful
while making people smile?

Making others laugh was something
she enjoyed and did without effort.

When the bell rang,
Grace picked up her bag
and slowly walked out the front
door to meet her mom.

As Grace climbed into the back seat,
she never looked at her mom, which was
very unusual for her. She loved talking
about her day at school.

Grace's mood worried her mother.
"I hope your day was well?"

"It was okay."

Mrs. Wilson didn't pressure Grace
to speak right away,
giving her some space

Sadly, Grace wasn't
the same person anymore.

Others noticed the change in Grace,
including her favorite teacher,
Mr. Williams. He pulled Jana to the side
and asked what was troubling Grace.

As Jana explained what happened in Mrs.
Henderson's class, Mr. Williams gave
Grace's mother a call to explain
what happened.

That afternoon, Grace mom picked
her up and drove into downtown Chicago.
To Grace's favorite place,
the Chicago Theatre.

As the two waited in their seat,
a beautiful woman hit the stage.

Within seconds, everyone was loudly
laughing. Grace was amazed as she saw
someone who had the same passion as
her to make others laugh!

As the show came to an end, Mrs. Wilson led her backstage to meet the comedian face-to-face.

"I heard about what happened with your teacher."

The woman smiled. "Don't worry. I had plenty of teachers like that too. But, keep laughing, keep smiling, and keep believing."

Grace smiled from ear to ear.

As she walked out, Grace broke away
from everyone, running towards
the stage.

She stood in the middle of the stage,
with her mother smiling in the audience,
and gave her best stand-up performance.

The more she told jokes, the more
her mother laughed.

As she glanced over, she noticed
the comedian clapping and cheering
her on too!

15 years later

Grace stood in her office, staring out the glass window that overlooked the water.

She thought about all the what-ifs. What if her mother didn't encourage her to be proud of who she was?

Would she have become the founder & CEO of the largest production company in Chicago or started a youth program teaching children to be confident in who they are?

Someone once told Grace, hoping to upset her, "They're all going to laugh at you."

They couldn't be more right . . .

They're all laughing, and she LOVED IT!

She's just a girl from the west side of Chicago, living her dreams.

Made in the USA
Monee, IL
11 August 2021